A DAY IN THE LIFE OF A
PILOT

THIS EDITION
Produced for DK by WonderLab Group LLC
Jennifer Emmett, Erica Green, Kate Hale, *Founders*

Editor Maya Myers; **Photography Editor** Kelley Miller; **Managing Editor** Rachel Houghton;
Designers Project Design Company; **Researcher** Michelle Harris; **Copy Editor** Lori Merritt;
Indexer Connie Binder; **Proofreader** Susan K. Hom; **Series Reading Specialist** Dr. Jennifer Albro;
Aviation Consultant Christopher Fleury

First American Edition, 2025
Published in the United States by DK Publishing, a division of Penguin Random House LLC
1745 Broadway, 20th Floor, New York, NY 10019

Copyright © 2025 Dorling Kindersley Limited
24 25 26 27 10 9 8 7 6 5 4 3 2 1
001–345392–April/2025

All rights reserved.
Without limiting the rights under the copyright reserved above, no part of this publication may be reproduced, stored in or introduced into a retrieval system, or transmitted, in any form, or by any means (electronic, mechanical, photocopying, recording, or otherwise), without the prior written permission of the copyright owner. Published in Great Britain by Dorling Kindersley Limited

A catalog record for this book is available from the Library of Congress.
HC ISBN: 978-0-5939-6239-8
PB ISBN: 978-0-5939-6238-1

DK books are available at special discounts when purchased in bulk for sales promotions, premiums, fund-raising, or educational use. For details, contact:
DK Publishing Special Markets, 1745 Broadway, 20th Floor, New York, NY 10019
SpecialSales@dk.com

Printed and bound in China
Super Readers Lexile® levels 310L to 490L
Lexile® is the registered trademark of MetaMetrics, Inc. Copyright © 2024 MetaMetrics, Inc. All rights reserved.

The publisher would like to thank the following for their kind permission to reproduce their images:
a=above; c=center; b=below; l=left; r=right; t=top; b/g=background
Dreamstime.com: Amaviael 11crb, Jaromír Chalabala 25, Chingyunsong 6, Ken Cole 18b, Dezzor 20-21, 24, Djama86 11b, Ivan Dudka 14-15, Aleksei Gorodenkov 19t, Antonio Guillem 28-29, Viacheslav Iacobchuk 16, Joyfull 4-5, Veniamin Kraskov 19br, Lightfieldstudiosprod 3, 9b, 27c, Carlos Lozano 26, Photographerlondon 29tr, Printezis 7tl, Rayp808 10, 28cra, Sergiy1975 11tr, Tea 13br, Tsvibrav 18br, 30bl (x2), Xaoc 7tr, Hongqi Zhang (aka Michael Zhang) 27br; **Fotolia:** Pekka Jaakkola / Luminis 9ca; **Getty Images / iStock:** Matthis Arrivet 8, E+ / 4FR 30cl, E+ / baona 12, 30cla, E+ / guvendemir 22, E+ / Portra 1, 17, 30tl, E+ / Tempura 13t, santofilme 20bl, Tuned_In 23; **Shutterstock.com:** schusterbauer.com 21cra, Olena Yakobchuk 6bn

Cover images: *Front:* **Dreamstime.com:** Designvectorpro (Background); **Getty Images / iStock:** E+ / Portra;
Back: **Dreamstime.com:** Macrovector cla, Pavel Voinau cra

www.dk.com

Level 1

A DAY IN THE LIFE OF A
PILOT

Paige Towler

Contents

6 What Does a Pilot Do?
10 Getting Ready
14 Safety First
18 Takeoff
22 In the Air

26 After the Flight
30 Glossary
31 Index
32 Quiz

What Does a Pilot Do?

Look! A plane! Who is flying the plane? Pilots!

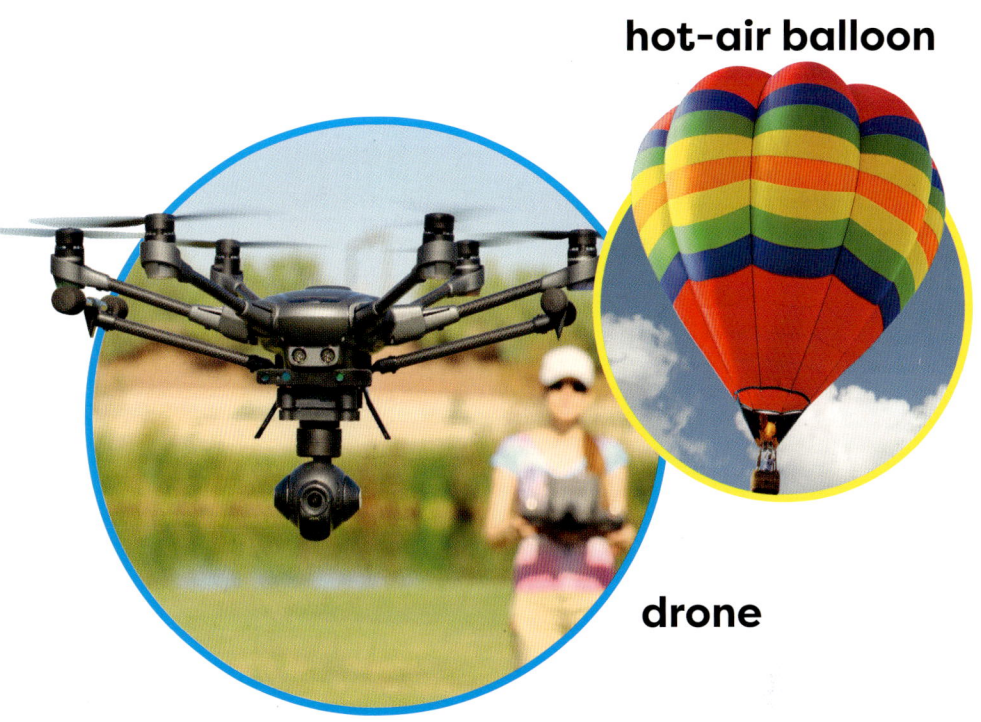

hot-air balloon

drone

A pilot is a person who flies an aircraft. There are many kinds of aircraft. Some pilots fly airplanes. Others fly helicopters. Some pilots even fly hot-air balloons! Pilots fly drones, too.

firefighting plane

Some pilots fly for fun. Others fly for work. Pilots use planes to do lots of different jobs.

Some planes can help put out wildfires. Some pilots fly fighter jets. Other pilots fly rescue planes.

Many pilots are airline pilots. They fly large planes that carry people and cargo.

Getting Ready

This pilot's uniform shows people she is in charge. She has four stripes on her sleeves. That means she is the captain of the airplane.

The pilot brings a flight bag. It holds things she will need for the flight.

An electronic tablet stores information.

A headset lets the pilot talk to people from the flight deck.

Sunglasses protect her eyes from the sun.

Airline pilots arrive for work at an airport. This is where airplanes take off and land.

This pilot greets her crew. The co-pilot and the captain will fly the plane together.

The cabin crew will take care of the passengers.

Safety First

The pilot checks the flight information. How many passengers will there be? How much fuel does the plane need?

The crew looks at the flight path. They check the weather. Being prepared keeps everyone safe.

This pilot checks the outside of the plane. He looks at the tires. He checks the engine.

These pilots sit in the flight deck. The flight deck has many controls. They help the pilot fly the plane. The pilots make sure everything is ready.

The two pilots work as a team. They double-check each other.

All set!

Takeoff

It's time for takeoff. The pilot drives the plane on the ground. This is called taxiing. She uses the tiller to steer. She moves the plane onto the runway. This is where planes take off and land.

The pilot talks to someone in air traffic control. They tell the pilot when it is safe to take off. Time to fly!

The pilot pushes on the throttle. **Vroom!** The throttle controls the engine. The plane goes very fast on the runway. Then, it rises into the air. The plane goes up, up, up!

The pilot lifts a lever. The plane pulls its wheels inside.

In the Air

The plane is flying up high now. This is called cruising.

This pilot uses the yoke to steer the plane. A screen in the flight deck gives him information while he flies. The chart tells him where to go.

yoke

This plane is almost at its destination. It is time to land. The pilot talks to air traffic control. She uses the throttle. It slows down the plane. She steers the plane lower. She lowers a lever to bring out the landing gear.

She makes sure the speed of the plane is just right. The plane lands on the runway. It taxis to the terminal. The terminal is part of the airport.

After the Flight

The passengers have arrived safely. This pilot checks the flight deck. He checks the outside of the plane.

These pilots and crew say goodbye. They walk into the terminal.

Most pilots fly more than one flight in a day! This pilot is on her way to another flight.

This pilot is heading home after a long flight.

This pilot will sleep at a hotel near the airport. Tomorrow, she will fly out again!

Glossary

flight deck
the control center of an airplane

terminal
a building where passengers and crew get on and off planes

throttle
the lever that controls a plane's engine

tiller
the part that steers the plane on the ground

yoke
the part that steers the plane in the air

Index

air traffic control 19, 24
airport 12, 25
crew 13
cruising 22
drones 7
fighter jets 8
firefighting plane 8
flight deck 11, 17, 23, 26
headset 11
helicopters 7
hot-air balloons 7
landing gear 24

rescue planes 8
runway 18, 20, 25
safety 14, 15, 19
sunglasses 11
takeoff 18
taxiing 18
terminal 25, 27
throttle 20, 24
tiller 18
uniform 10
wheels 21
yoke 23

Quiz

Answer the questions to see what you have learned. Check your answers with an adult.

1. What are some kinds of aircraft that pilots fly?
2. Who has four stripes on their pilot uniform?
3. What is it called when the pilot steers a plane on the runway?
4. What is it called when the plane is flying high in the sky?
5. True or False: Pilots never fly more than one flight per day.

1. Passenger planes, fighter jets, helicopters, hot-air balloons
2. The captain 3. Taxiing 4. Cruising 5. False